The Visual Guide to

Asperger's Syndrome and Executive Function

by Alis Rowe

Also by Alis Rowe

One Lonely Mind
978-0-9562693-0-0

The Girl with the Curly Hair - Asperger's and Me
978-0-9562693-2-4

The 1st Comic Book
978-0-9562693-1-7

The 2nd Comic Book
978-0-9562693-4-8

The 3rd Comic Book
978-0-9562693-3-1

The 4th Comic Book
978-15086839-7-1

The 5th Comic Book
978-15309879-3-1

Websites:
www.thegirlwiththecurlyhair.co.uk
www.thecurlyhairconsultancy.com
www.theliftingplace.com

Social Media:
www.facebook.com/thegirlwiththecurlyhair
www.twitter.com/curlyhairedalis

The Visual Guide to

Asperger's Syndrome and Executive Function

by Alis Rowe

Lonely Mind Books
London

For people on the autism spectrum and the people around them

hello

People with Autism Spectrum Disorder (ASD) tend to have problems with their executive function. It can make us very slow, rigid, forgetful, disorganised... and can make us miss solutions to even the most simple problems.

I don't think I was aware of just how impaired I was by executive function until my lifestyle changed, and now I'm probably more productive and efficient than ever!

I haven't done one thing in particular. I've made a lot of quite simple and straightforward changes in my day to day life. I take a very holistic approach in which I take into account life as a whole.

I hope the strategies in this book help you to become more productive too!

Alis aka The Girl with the Curly Hair

Contents

p11   **What is executive function?**

p41   **How to improve executive function**

What is executive function?

Executive function is a set of mental skills that help people get things done

These skills are controlled by an area in the brain called the frontal lobe

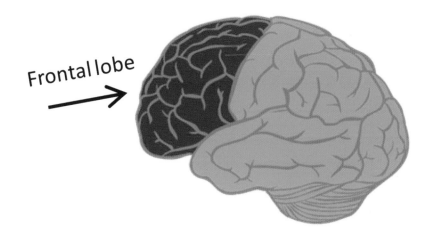

Frontal lobe →

It is thought that people on the autistic spectrum have impaired executive function

What are some of the things that executive function is responsible for?

EXECUTIVE FUNCTION

WORKING MEMORY

FLEXIBLE THINKING

ORGANISATION

STARTING TASKS

CONTROLLING IMPULSES

REGULATING EMOTIONS

SELF-MONITORING

PLANNING AND PRIORITISING

In this book The Girl with the Curly Hair has made the assumption that neurotypical people have good executive function and autistic people have impaired executive function

(This is for simplicity because some neurotypical people have difficulties with executive function... we all know people who are poor at planning, disorganised and forgetful, for example!)

Aware and unaware thoughts

The Girl with the Curly Hair proposes that there are two main styles of thinking:

1) thoughts that you are aware of, and
2) thoughts that you are unaware of, that run automatically

The Girl with the Curly Hair thinks therefore, that non-autistic thinking is like this:

Neurotypical people have a lot of unaware thoughts

Most of the things they do are controlled through these unaware thoughts

This means that most things get done at no extra, conscious or additional effort

Executive function is quite an unaware thing – it runs in the background

The Girl with the Curly Hair thinks that autistic thinking is like this:

The Girl with the Curly Hair has a large number of thoughts that she is aware of

She feels like she is always thinking

She has to think very hard about everything she does

Executive function is a conscious thing

The Girl with the Curly Hair feels that every thought and behaviour she has, is very conscious

For example, she may not even know how she is feeling until she stops and thinks about it

She can almost feel the cogs in her brain working!

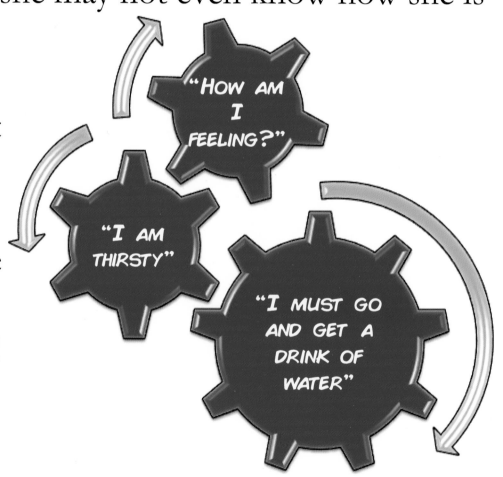

Executive function is like a wonderful machine – every time a task needs to be done the cog wheels all start turning

For neurotypical people, any task they have to do, the cog wheels fit together smoothly and quickly

For autistic people, any task they have to do, the cog wheels are misshapen or missing, or perhaps it just takes a long time for them to start turning

Consequences of impaired executive function

When a person has impaired executive function, it means they have trouble getting things done and/or that they might be very slow to do things

But another big consequence is that all that extra thinking and effort required to do things means more energy is being used and the person gets very, very tired

23

The CBT (Cognitive Behavioural Therapy) model can be applied to executive function

If we are thinking very hard and our cogs are going into overdrive, this energy will have an effect on our mood

It's not surprising that The Girl with the Curly Hair feels tired, stressed, overwhelmed, frustrated and impatient a lot of the time

These feelings might consequently show in her behaviour

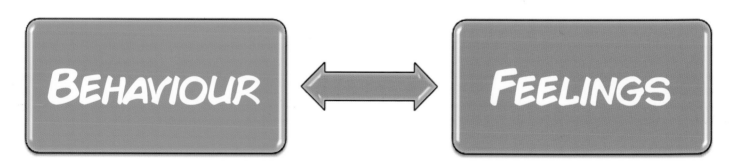

For example, The Girl with the Curly Hair finds it difficult to remember what to take with her every time she leaves her house. She has to check, double and triple check she's got everything, every single time

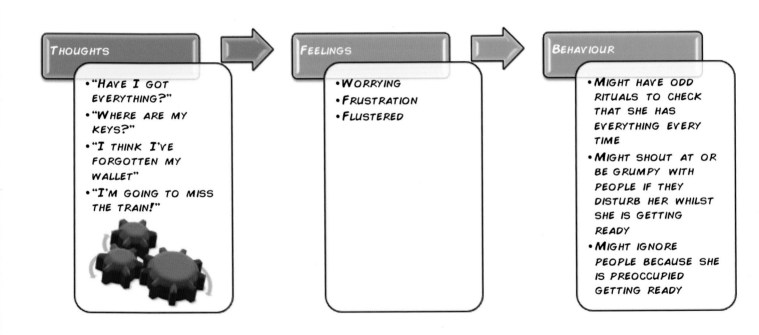

THOUGHTS
- "HAVE I GOT EVERYTHING?"
- "WHERE ARE MY KEYS?"
- "I THINK I'VE FORGOTTEN MY WALLET"
- "I'M GOING TO MISS THE TRAIN!"

FEELINGS
- WORRYING
- FRUSTRATION
- FLUSTERED

BEHAVIOUR
- MIGHT HAVE ODD RITUALS TO CHECK THAT SHE HAS EVERYTHING EVERY TIME
- MIGHT SHOUT AT OR BE GRUMPY WITH PEOPLE IF THEY DISTURB HER WHILST SHE IS GETTING READY
- MIGHT IGNORE PEOPLE BECAUSE SHE IS PREOCCUPIED GETTING READY

The table on the next page describes some examples of the different skills of executive function (there are also lots more!)

Autistic people are likely to find many of these skills very difficult

Skill	This means:
Working memory	Retaining distinct bits of information over short periods of time
Flexible thinking	Changing one's response depending on what the situation has called for
Organisation	Foreseeing the steps in the right order to achieve what needs to be done
Starting tasks	Acting out the first step of something
Controlling impulses	Resisting doing something because it's inappropriate or unproductive
Regulating emotions	The ability to remain calm or to react sensibly
Planning and prioritising	Deciding and working on the first or most important step whilst resisting other steps

Executive function is required for even very simple tasks

Let's now look at the example of making a cup of tea and see if we can identify the executive function skills

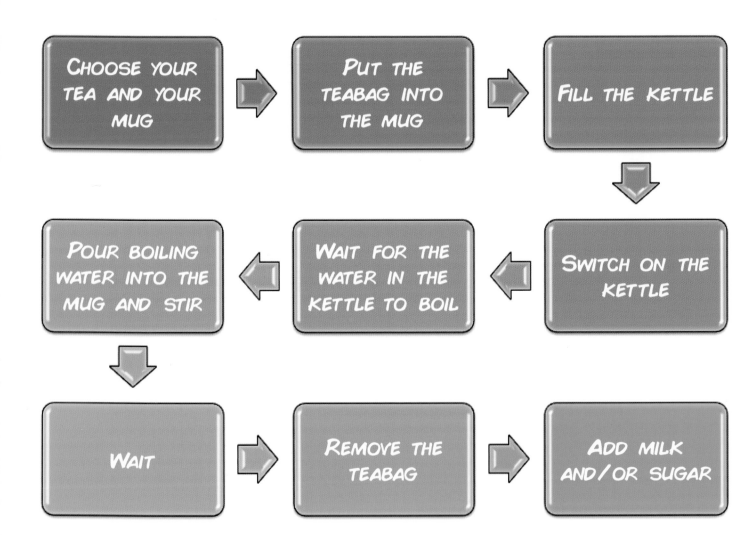

Skill	Relevance to making a cup of tea
Working memory	Required the entire time to remember what steps have been done and what has to be done next – for example, don't put two teabags in the mug and don't pour the kettle unless it has boiled!
Flexible thinking	What to do if there's no milk, no teabags, or if there are no clean mugs?
Organisation	Making the tea in the right order and at the right time - getting out a mug, getting out the milk and sugar, filling the kettle, waiting for the water to boil before pouring it, etc.
Starting tasks	You've decided to make a cup of tea or someone has asked you to make them a cup of tea
Controlling impulses	You have to remain focused until the tea has been made and not get distracted doing something else
Regulating emotions	Staying calm until the tea has been made
Planning	Thinking about making a cup of tea and how to make it, because you have identified that you want one or someone else wants one

That's just for making a cup of tea!

Imagine all the executive function that's required for more complicated or longer tasks

Most neurotypical people don't have to think very much when they make a cup of tea or for other things they do, but autistic people are likely to always be thinking very hard

Here are a couple of other examples of situations where executive function is required

What happens when a neurotypical person goes to brush their teeth in the morning and finds that there is no toothpaste? Executive function kicks in!

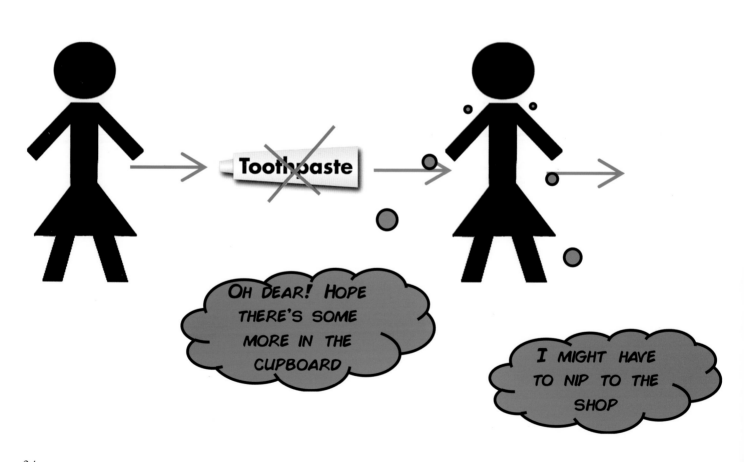

What happens when The Girl with the Curly Hair goes to brush her teeth in the morning and finds that there is no toothpaste? Executive function fails!

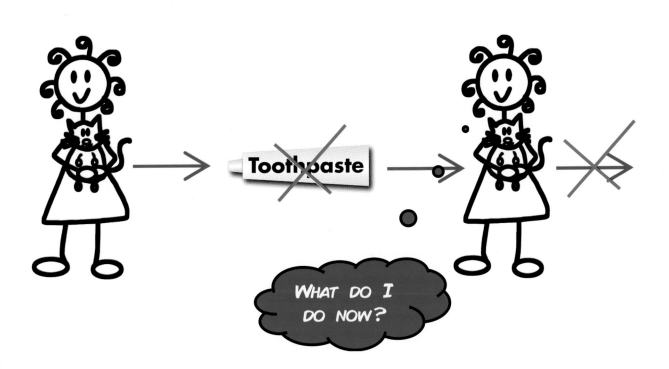

What happens when a neurotypical person goes to college and finds a note on the door that says 'class is cancelled'? Executive function kicks in!

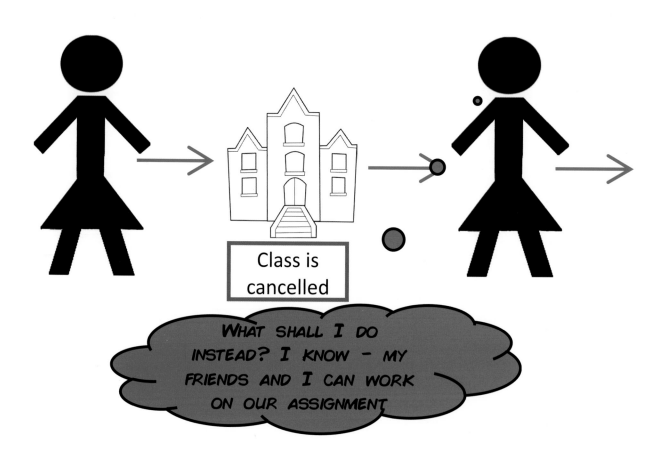

What happens when The Girl with the Curly Hair goes to college and finds a note on the door that says class is cancelled? Executive function fails!

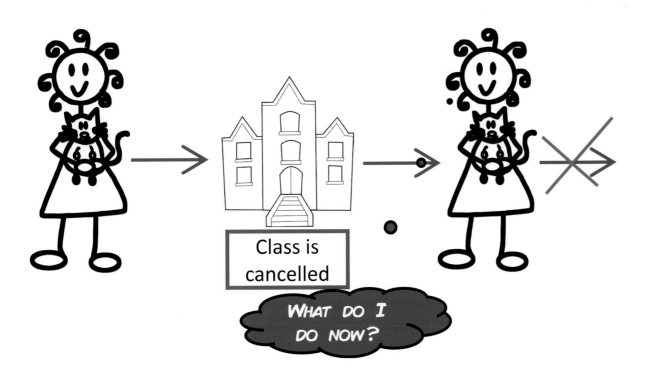

She actually ends up wandering around aimlessly for the whole hour before her next lesson

The Freeze Response

When executive function is stressed, it can cause a person to 'freeze' and not be able to do the next step

The cogs in the brain come to a halt

Mum chats to The Girl with the Curly Hair when she gets home from college that day:

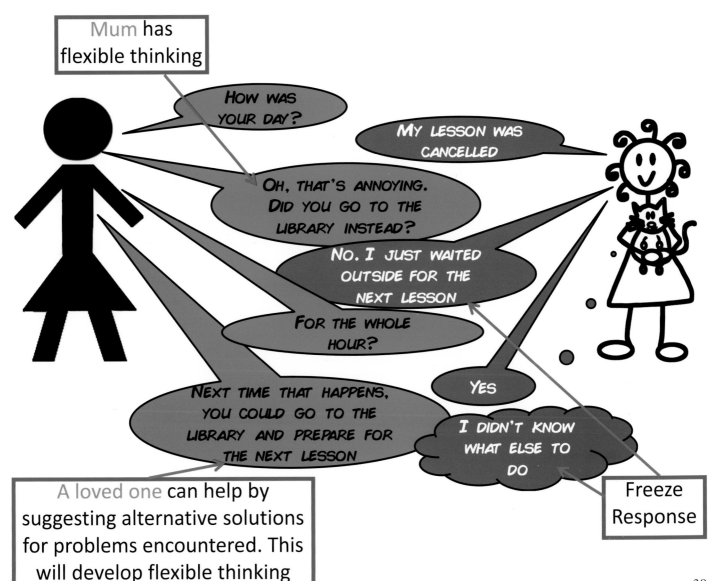

Mum has flexible thinking

HOW WAS YOUR DAY?

MY LESSON WAS CANCELLED

OH, THAT'S ANNOYING. DID YOU GO TO THE LIBRARY INSTEAD?

NO. I JUST WAITED OUTSIDE FOR THE NEXT LESSON

FOR THE WHOLE HOUR?

YES

NEXT TIME THAT HAPPENS, YOU COULD GO TO THE LIBRARY AND PREPARE FOR THE NEXT LESSON

I DIDN'T KNOW WHAT ELSE TO DO

A loved one can help by suggesting alternative solutions for problems encountered. This will develop flexible thinking

Freeze Response

How to improve executive function

There are lots of things people can do to improve their executive function – here are some techniques that The Girl with the Curly Hair has learned that really help her

Routines

SOME PEOPLE THINK THAT I AM TOO RIGID AND ANXIOUS ABOUT WHAT'S ON MY AGENDA AND THAT I'M "ALL ABOUT TIMES AND SCHEDULES"

THE THING IS, I'M LIKE THIS BECAUSE MY ROUTINES **ENABLE** ME TO DO THINGS. IF I DIDN'T HAVE ROUTINES, NOTHING WOULD GET DONE!

If you think about it, a routine is really just a habit

What's the good thing about habits? People don't even have to think about them – they just do them. This is very efficient and reduces mental energy

So for The Girl with the Curly Hair, creating and maintaining her routines is a really good way of reducing the amount of thinking she has to do and improves her executive function

Examples of habits:

Hourly	Daily	Weekly
Drinking a glass of water*	Brushing my teeth	Washing my clothes
Going to the toilet*	Walking the dog	Vacuuming the house
Stretching my legs	Going out for a cup of coffee	Tidying my room

*We included these in because it may be a strategy for autistic people who are not able to recognise when they need to go to the toilet or when they are thirsty

All of these things require an enormous number of executive function skills to work together. They can be really hard to do. However, one trick that The Girl with the Curly Hair has learned is to do them often enough, regularly, and once she's done things enough, she doesn't have to think about them any more and they are easy

Routines are really important in enabling things to get done. A routine means that eventually a person will automatically know what they need to do rather than have to always be thinking about it

This will free up some space inside the head for thinking about other things!

Advance notice

Any disruption or change to a plan can turn a task from easy to hard, as more executive function skills are required to problem solve and adapt to the change

This is why it's important to try to ensure things go to plan. If there are any changes, let the person know in advance. It gives them time to think about the consequences of the changes ahead of time rather than in the moment

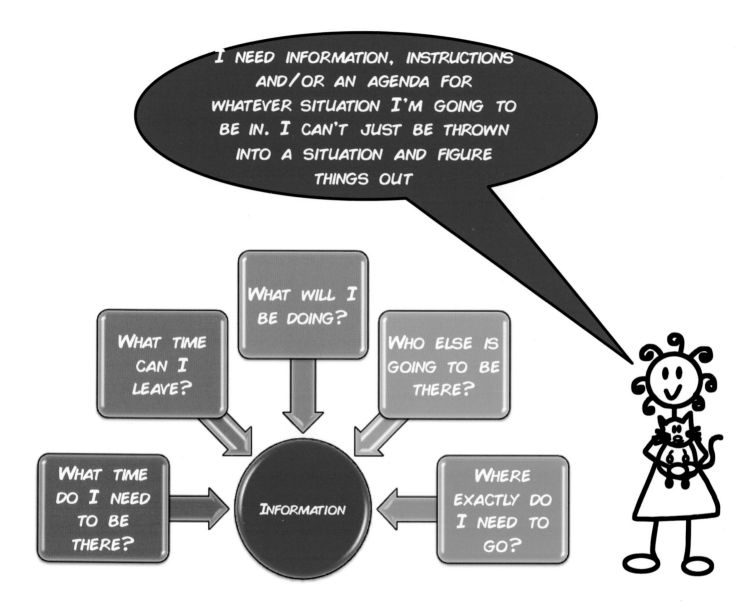

Having this information is important, not just because it makes someone less anxious, but it enables them ahead of time to think about what might be different or what could go wrong. Then they can think about what they would do if something was different or did go wrong

For example, thinking about some of the things that could be different or go wrong in advance of the dental appointment (see next page) and coming up with strategies for these things can mean the person will be better equipped to deal with anything should it happen - this also limits the likelihood of the freeze response happening

Neurotypical people probably don't have sorts of things, as their executive function figure out things automatically

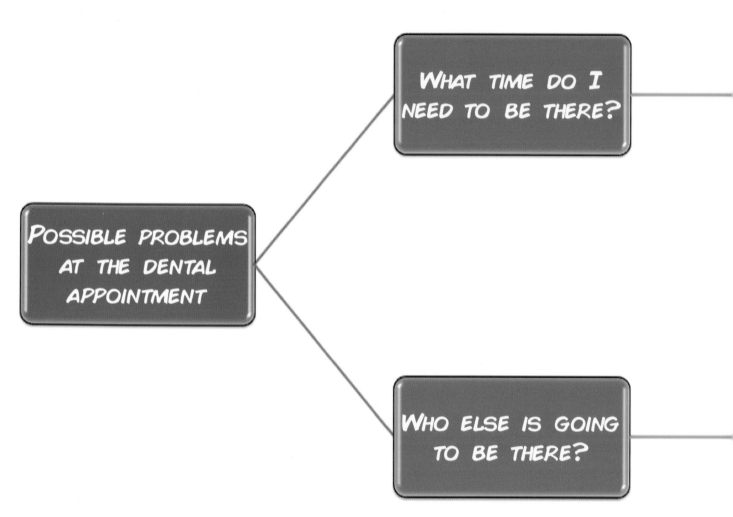

POSSIBLE PROBLEMS AT THE DENTAL APPOINTMENT

WHAT TIME DO I NEED TO BE THERE?

WHO ELSE IS GOING TO BE THERE?

to think as much about these is good enough to

I NEED TO BE THERE AT 10:00

THE BUS COULD BE LATE

THE APPOINTMENT MIGHT NOT START ON TIME

I MIGHT FORGET MY BUS PASS

THE DENTIST AND THE DENTAL NURSE WILL BE THERE

IT COULD BE A DIFFERENT DENTIST

THERE COULD BE LOTS OF SMALL TALK

Thinking and talking about different scenarios and outcomes is really important

You can do this for any aspect of life

It can improve 'flexible thinking' which is arguably one of the most impairing parts of ASD

What could happen when The Girl with the Curly Hair goes to brush her teeth? What could some solutions for these things be? It's helpful to think about alternatives on your own as well as with others

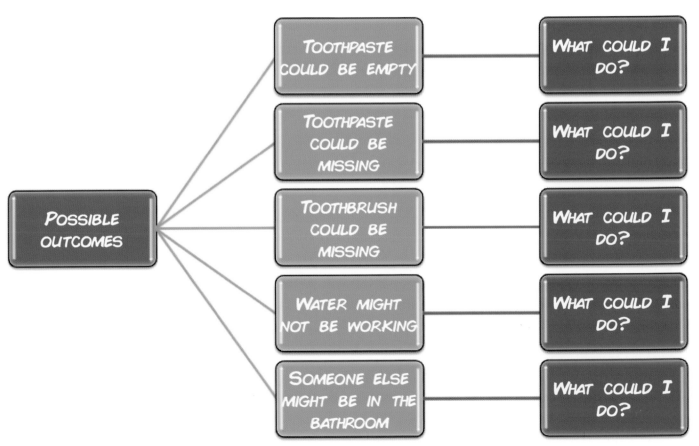

Looking at things from other people's perspectives

Looking at things from different people's perspectives is really important in developing 'theory of mind' (a part of flexible thinking). Good theory of mind is essential for having strong relationships with other people

The Girl with the Curly Hair likes to keep a journal in which she thinks about situations that have happened from different points of view, for example:

The Girl with the Curly Hair feels anxious and cross

Friend: Could be anxiously rushing to be on time, might not have even noticed the time, someone bumped into them on their way and they got held up...

The Girl with the Curly Hair feels anxious, worried, or thinks she's done something wrong.

Boss: Needs some work doing, wants to show her something new, wants to bring up a problem that he knows she would know how to solve

The Girl with the Curly Hair feels excited because she's making space to make her house even bigger!

Friend: Wants to carry on building her own house, was building something fantastic, is hurt that The Girl with the Curly Hair didn't consider her actions, thinks she is selfish

Minimising transitions

Transitions are moving from one thing to another and can include…

Outside ⟷ Inside
Activity 1 ⟶ Activity 2
Room A ⟶ Room B

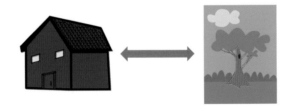

Transitions require executive function such as the ability to stop something and begin another; or getting yourself organised to do something different or go somewhere different

One tip that The Girl with the Curly Hair has found useful is to keep the number of transitions she does each day to a minimum. For example her old life was a bit more like this:

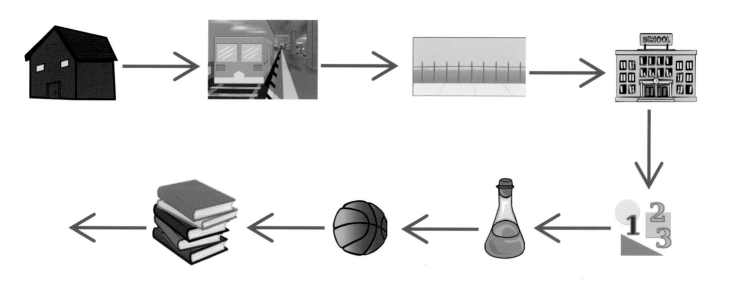

That's an enormous number of transitions!

She's left her house, got on the train, travelled on the train, walked to school, done Maths, English, Science, P.E. (no doubt also had lunch and break time), walked back to the station, got back on the train and gone home again

When you think of how many different activities and environments she has exposed herself to, you can think about the enormous amount of executive function processes that have been used!

University was a lot better because the number of transitions she had to do was much less:

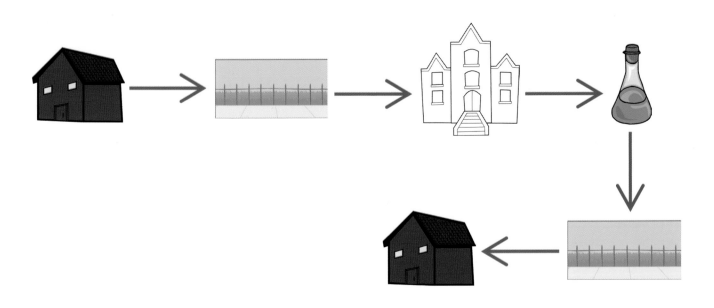

She used to walk there; she only did one subject (Chemistry) and sometimes there were just one or two lessons in a day

Working from home has even less transitions as she only really has to work and go out once to walk the dog!

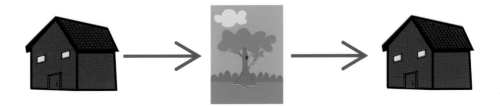

What you consider to be a significant transition is a personal thing

- Some people will cope fine with lots of different environments
- Some people will cope fine with lots of different tasks
- A person might find certain transitions more difficult than others

It is a good idea however, to be aware of transitions and try to think of ways they could be reduced and see if it makes a positive difference to your abilities and energy levels

Tips to minimise transitions:

WEAR VERSATILE CLOTHES SO YOU DON'T HAVE TO CHANGE AS MUCH THROUGHOUT THE DAY/WEEK

ONLY MAKE THE TRANSITION OF HOME -> OUT ONCE PER DAY (SO DO ALL THINGS OUTSIDE OF THE HOUSE AT ONCE)

ONLY DO ONE THING AT A TIME WHEN OUT

MEET PEOPLE AND DO THINGS CLOSE TO HOME TO MINIMISE TRAVELLING ENVIRONMENTS

MINIMISE THE TYPE OF TRANSPORT TAKEN ON ONE JOURNEY (E.G. CAN THE WHOLE JOURNEY BE DONE BY BUS RATHER THAN TRAIN+TUBE+BUS?)

CUT DOWN ON YOUR EXTRACURRICULAR ACTIVITIES

HAVE ONLY ONE MAIN TASK TO DO A DAY

TAKE BREAKS THROUGHOUT THE DAY IN THE SAME PHYSICAL SPACE

Having a less busy life

A life that is busy or busier times of the day mean there is a demand on executive function

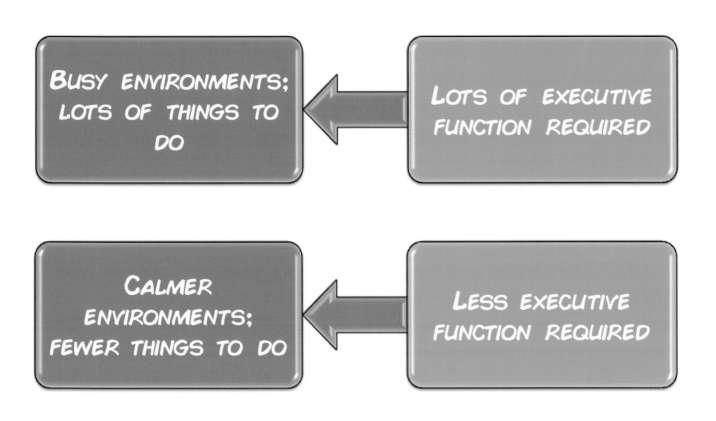

Pacing out your day might improve executive function

Some people notice that they really struggle at certain times of the day more than others, for example the morning

This could be because more things need to be thought about and done at this time (waking up on time, getting ready, having breakfast, catching the train…)

Another tip therefore, may be getting things ready the night before, so that less needs to be done and thought about in the morning

Getting ready for work example:

The Girl with the Curly Hair used to find getting ready for work in the morning a bit too hectic

She decided to move some of the tasks that she was doing in the morning to the night before, and it really helped

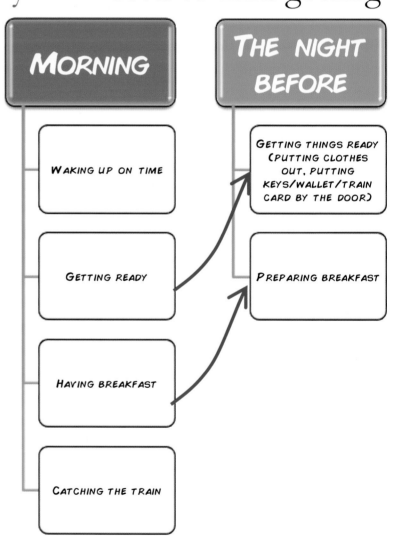

Find the time of day that suits you best

The time of day that something is done may have an impact on your executive function

Many people find they have a higher attention span and find things easier if they are done in the morning when they are least tired. Some people prefer to work on things at night

Some people think they're not morning people but they do actually have the most attention at this time!

70

Doing the same things

Being given decisions or being faced with lots of options can be difficult because it means there's a lot of information to think about, all putting stress on executive function

Often just making the same choice every time is a way to reduce the amount of work the brain has to do!

Making the same choice every time is just easier...

Making other choices tends to mean this happens...

If a choice does have to be made, it's helpful to keep the options minimal...

Having a minimal number of ideas

The Girl with the Curly Hair doesn't like having a lot of ideas for the same reasons… there just becomes too much to think about. She hates to brainstorm!

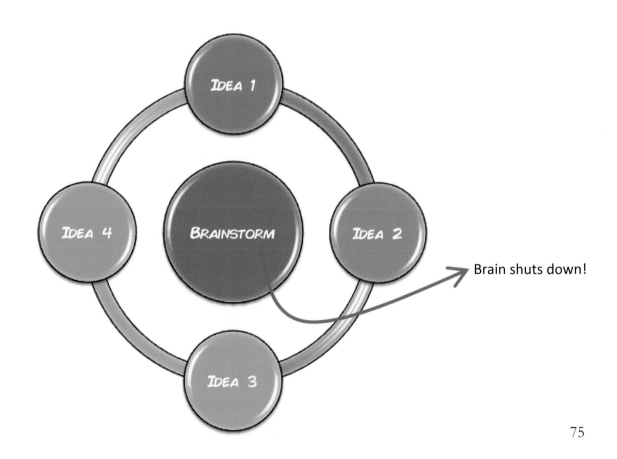

Ideas for her are too abstract

She doesn't find having lots of ideas helpful. She doesn't actually like having ideas because of the volume of work on the brain. Just one idea that becomes reality is fine for her and then she will move on to another idea if she wants to…

Or if someone else wants to work on another idea and she's able to delegate, that works!

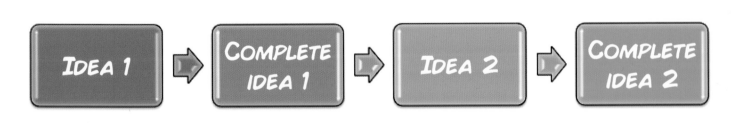

Doing one thing at a time helps

The Girl with the Curly Hair likes to do one thing at a time. She likes to use the analogy in Physics studies of simultaneous vs sequential processing:

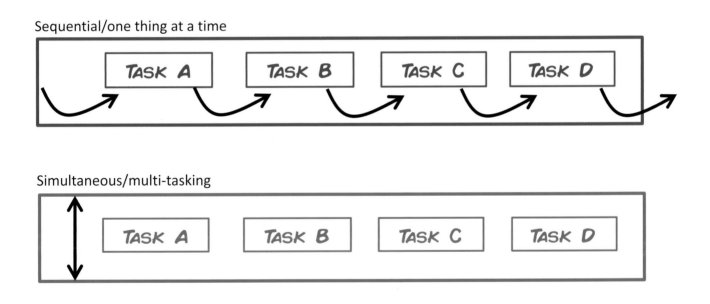

Perhaps neurotypical people are more capable of doing simultaneous processing/multi-tasking

Communicating

To improve executive function, talking about one topic at a time, or having a structure to a conversation can really help

Using short sentences, clear, concise language, making obvious time gaps for questions and answers, and clearly confirming when a topic has finished being discussed, are all helpful things for autistic people when they are communicating

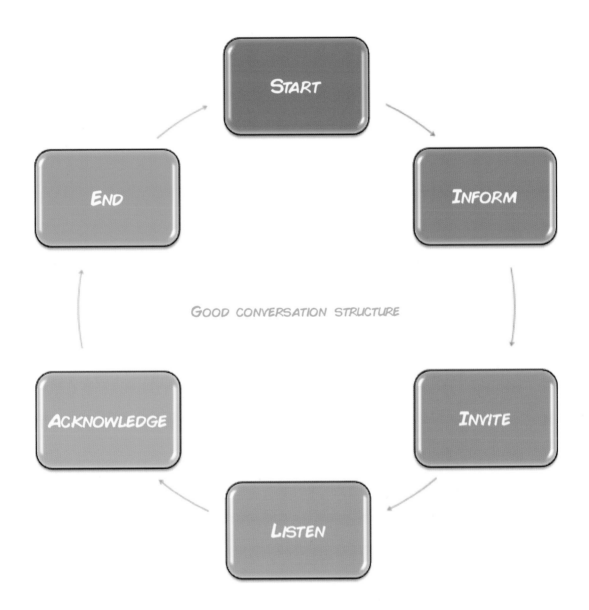

Good conversation structure

Lots of alone time

Alone time isn't just needed to recharge from socialising, it's also needed to recharge executive function and to use executive function, without additional stressors

If other people are around, the person has to use additional executive function to think about that person's needs and behaviour and how they perhaps ought to be behaving in front of those people, instead of being able to focus wholly on their own thoughts and what they are doing

An autistic person might also need to be on their own in order to be able to figure out how to do a task so that they can do it at their own pace and adapt it to their way of thinking

Having other people instructing how a task needs to be done, or even just being present, can hinder an individual's learning

Agendas are helpful

It's important to always have an agenda for the day. The Girl with the Curly Hair likes to have her daily schedule prepared the night before, so that she always wakes up already knowing what she's going to be doing (this also gives her motivation to get up – very important in times of depression and severe anxiety)

Different types of agendas will work for different people

Some people like lists with no particular time or order, some people need times, some people need sequences

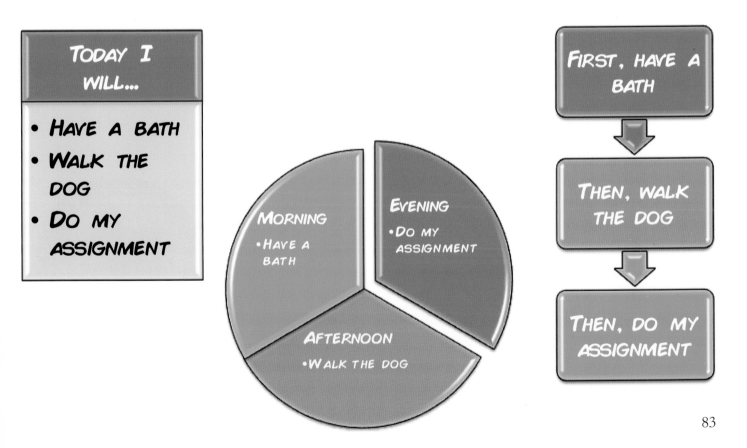

Make time visible

Some autistic people are 'time-blind' – a good trick to deal with this is to make time very visible everywhere

Use timers, clocks, countdowns… they are all helpful ways of making the time be seen

Frequent breaks

Breaks throughout the day and throughout the week can give the brain a chance to recharge and the executive function can have a chance to recharge!

Perhaps sometimes those cog wheels get a bit heated and swollen from being overworked and a break resets them back to their original size, making it more likely they'll turn again!

Regular physical activity

Physical activity gets blood moving to the brain, which helps in improving executive function!

Being active throughout the day is a good thing for anyone - you can do it by using the stairs instead of the lift, parking furthest away from the entrance to the shop, getting off the bus a stop early, going for walks on your lunch break... etc.

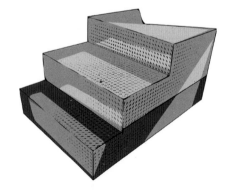

Sport and exercise are good at improving certain executive function skills, for example:

• motor coordination between the brain and body
• working memory, if following a particular instruction or sequence
• planning and organisation are required if a person has to fit exercise into their working day
• many skills have to be used if a person has to think about what sort of exercises they will need to do if they want to reach their fitness goals

Try to find an exercise you really, really like (The Girl with the Curly Hair likes weightlifting)

Break tasks down

Some tasks might be perceived as very big

Breaking tasks down reduces this perception of a high workload

It also gives the person a chance to practice stopping and starting something else and transitioning

Accomplishing each smaller task can also be really rewarding (and good for people who benefit from having rewards and where the bigger goal might take too long for them to wait for the reward)

Example: The Girl with the Curly Hair wants to create a website

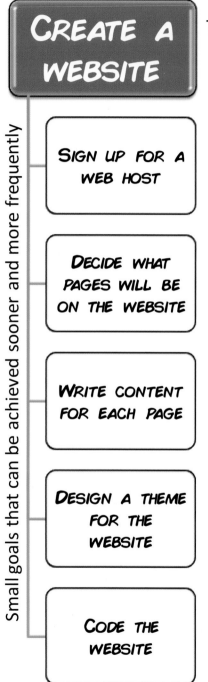

CREATE A WEBSITE

The big goal which could take a few weeks or months to achieve

Small goals that can be achieved sooner and more frequently

SIGN UP FOR A WEB HOST

DECIDE WHAT PAGES WILL BE ON THE WEBSITE

WRITE CONTENT FOR EACH PAGE

DESIGN A THEME FOR THE WEBSITE

CODE THE WEBSITE

Understanding the reason for things

Understanding why something has to be done might make someone more likely to do it

Understanding the negative consequences if they don't do it may make someone more likely to do the task

Task	Why it's important	What will happen if I don't do it
Having a bath and washing my hair	It's hygienic; it's pleasant for other people	I could get sick; people won't like being around me; my hair will feel knotty and greasy which I hate
Drinking water	To stay hydrated and to keep my body functioning correctly	I could get ill

Allowing extra time

Accepting that it might take a person longer to do something, especially the first time they do it

But once they've found their own method or have built a routine, they'll probably be able to do it very quickly and efficiently

They have to give themselves time and be patient with themselves; and other people have to be patient with them and give them that extra time

Presenting or looking at information in another format

You can improve executive function by changing the way that information is presented, for example:

Bullet points, white space, pictures, videos, showing someone how to do something, using actions related to learning (for example, counting on your fingers is a way many people learned and remembered how to count)

Individuals can benefit from working out what type of learner they are and adapting information to fit their preferred learning style. The VAK model* suggests there are 4 main styles of learning:

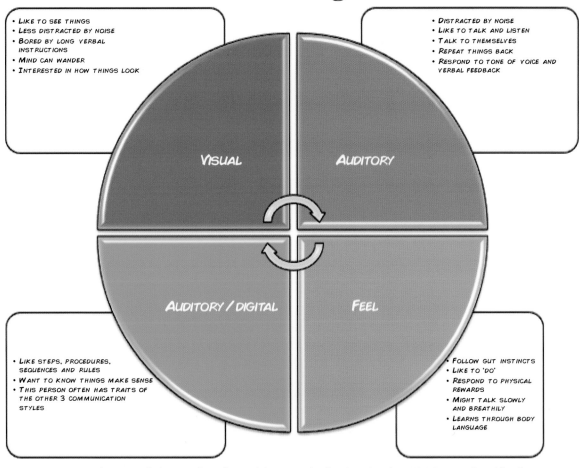

- LIKE TO SEE THINGS
- LESS DISTRACTED BY NOISE
- BORED BY LONG VERBAL INSTRUCTIONS
- MIND CAN WANDER
- INTERESTED IN HOW THINGS LOOK

- DISTRACTED BY NOISE
- LIKE TO TALK AND LISTEN
- TALK TO THEMSELVES
- REPEAT THINGS BACK
- RESPOND TO TONE OF VOICE AND VERBAL FEEDBACK

VISUAL

AUDITORY

AUDITORY / DIGITAL

FEEL

- LIKE STEPS, PROCEDURES, SEQUENCES AND RULES
- WANT TO KNOW THINGS MAKE SENSE
- THIS PERSON OFTEN HAS TRAITS OF THE OTHER 3 COMMUNICATION STYLES

- FOLLOW GUT INSTINCTS
- LIKE TO 'DO'
- RESPOND TO PHYSICAL REWARDS
- MIGHT TALK SLOWLY AND BREATHILY
- LEARNS THROUGH BODY LANGUAGE

*The VAK Learning Styles Model was developed by psychologists in the 1920s to classify the most common ways that people learn

THERE IS NO POINT TELLING ME WHAT I WILL NEED TO DO. I PROBABLY WON'T UNDERSTAND AND WON'T REMEMBER

BUT WRITE ME DOWN A LIST AND I WILL DO IT

Be aware of the environment

Autistic people are likely to feel uncomfortable and distracted by the sensory information (sounds, smells, lights, etc.) in their environments

Keeping things minimal is important – an uncluttered workspace, minimal or undistracting visuals and smells, fewer people, quieter places, less chaos, a person having their own space… etc.

The Girl with the Curly Hair thinks that neurotypical people have a filter in their brain that allows them to filter out a lot of sensory information

For example, when she was in a lesson at school, she found it hard to concentrate because of the sensations around her

Her neurotypical classmates weren't bothered by these things and could concentrate on what the teacher was teaching because their brains were filtering out all the unpleasant, unnecessary and irrelevant things

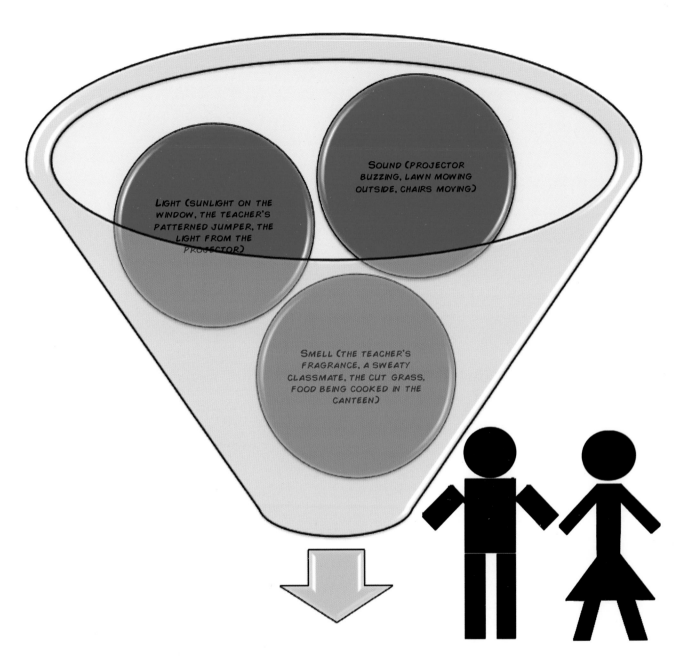

LIGHT (SUNLIGHT ON THE WINDOW, THE TEACHER'S PATTERNED JUMPER, THE LIGHT FROM THE PROJECTOR)

SOUND (PROJECTOR BUZZING, LAWN MOWING OUTSIDE, CHAIRS MOVING)

SMELL (THE TEACHER'S FRAGRANCE, A SWEATY CLASSMATE, THE CUT GRASS, FOOD BEING COOKED IN THE CANTEEN)

WHAT THE TEACHER IS TEACHING

Present information in an uncluttered way

WRITTEN:

- SHORT, CONCISE SENTENCES
- MAKE USE OF WHITE SPACE
- USE PARAGRAPHS
- USE BULLET POINTS
- INCLUDE PICTURES AND DIAGRAMS
- INCLUDE SOME COLOUR

VERBALLY:

- SHORT, CONCISE SENTENCES
- DON'T SPEAK TOO FAST
- KEEP ON TOPIC
- GET TO THE POINT
- DIRECT QUESTIONS OR STATEMENTS

The STOP practice

STOP is a practice used in Mindfulness that helps people be aware of themselves and their environments. Doing this throughout the day can help someone be more aware of their emotions and their behaviour (both really important aspects of executive function):

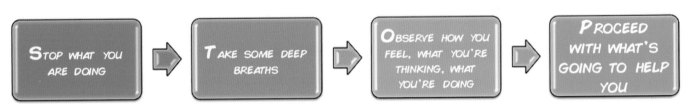

The Girl with the Curly Hair sets a timer on her phone every hour to check in with herself and monitor whether her behaviour is matching her goals, and whether her behaviour is positively helping her emotions

The first time something is done, try to ensure it goes well

A person who has done something repeatedly may have a greater ability to cope with changes in the situation, as opposed someone who is doing it for the first time

Doing anything for the first time requires an enormous amount of executive function, so it's important to try and ensure it goes as successfully as possible

Summary

Autistic people are likely to have trouble doing things due to impaired executive function

It can be the reason for many 'challenging behaviours' such as a person not doing something correctly, forgetting things, being rigid about the way something is done, or being very slow

Executive function is responsible for so many things including: planning, organising, remembering, coordinating our brains and body, adjusting to change, problem solving and staying focused

Most tasks require lots of different executive function skills so it might be most helpful to improve executive function as a whole

This book takes a holistic approach and suggests simple, effective strategies to help *anyone* be more productive!

Many thanks for reading

Other books in The Visual Guides series at the time of writing:

Asperger's Syndrome
Asperger's Syndrome: Meltdowns and Shutdowns
Asperger's Syndrome in 5-8 Year Olds
Asperger's Syndrome in 8-11 Year Olds
Asperger's Syndrome in 13-16 Year Olds
Asperger's Syndrome in 16-18 Year Olds
Asperger's Syndrome: Socialising & Social Energy
Asperger's Syndrome and Anxiety
Asperger's Syndrome: Helping Siblings
Asperger's Syndrome and Puberty
Asperger's Syndrome: Meltdowns and Shutdowns (2)
Adapting Health Therapies for People on the Autism Spectrum
Asperger's Syndrome and Emotions
Asperger's Syndrome: Understanding Each Other (For ASD/NT Couples)

New titles are continually being produced so keep an eye out!